Body Art

by Helen Orme

D0718760

Trailblazers

Body Art
by Helen Orme
Educational consultant: Helen Bird

Illustrated by Øivind Hovland

Published by Ransom Publishing Ltd.
51 Southgate Street, Winchester, Hants. SO23 9EH
www.ransom.co.uk

ISBN   978 184167 808 5
First published in 2009

Body Art

Contents

Body
Art

Get
the
facts

What is body art?

Body art is about making yourself look different.

jewellery

Some people decorate themselves with jewellery.

piercing

Sometimes people pierce parts of their body so they can wear jewels or other decorations.

Many people pierce their ears. Others pierce their noses and lips.

Some people pierce in even more painful places!

tattoos

Tattoos are popular with people all over the world. Sometimes these patterns are permanent. But they can be painted on.

Mehndi designs, often called henna tattoos, have been used in India for thousands of years. They are often used during marriage ceremonies.

face paint

Children paint their faces at special events.

Face painting is popular too.

Some football fans like to show which teams they support.

Painting your face might make it hard for your enemies to spot you.

7

Is body art a new idea?

Even people who lived thousands of years ago decorated their bodies.

The **ancient Egyptians** wore eye make-up.

They made their eye make-up from powdered **minerals** mixed with animal fat.

Tattoos sometimes showed how important a person was.

The oldest tattoos we have seen are on **Oetzi the ice-man**. Oetzi is the mummy of a man who lived 4,000 years ago. His body was found in the Alps.

Many people had tattoos on their **faces** and **hands**.

Sailors often had tattoos. They liked to show they had visited lots of different countries.

In some countries **scar patterns** were sometimes used to show that a person was an adult.

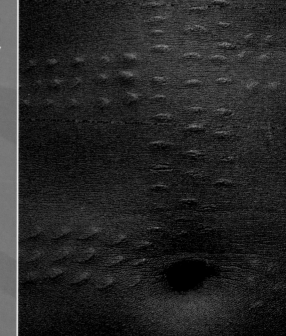

A scar pattern is made by **cutting**, then rubbing in something which will cause the healing skin to puff up.

The scars were sometimes coloured by **rubbing in ashes** or **soil**.

9

Looking **good**

All women like to carry their make-up around with them.

This is a very old make-up case.

It would have been owned by someone very rich.

Roman ladies used make-up that was similar to the things we use today.

This jar of cream was found in a Roman coffin.

You can see the owner's finger marks.

Today women use **cosmetics** similar to those used by women thousands of years ago. But there is **more choice** now.

Hair can be dyed in lots of different colours and worn in many different styles.

We have **lipsticks** and eye make-up in hundreds of different shades. Women can use **glitter** on their faces and bodies.

Going to extremes

Some societies wanted more than just painted designs on their bodies. They changed their **body shape**.

These people think that **long flat heads** look good.

Babies have their heads tightly wrapped to make them grow like this.

Some people in Europe did this too. In parts of **France**, head-binding was done until the 19th century.

In **China**, from the 10th century until the beginning of the 20th century, women wanted **very small feet**.

Baby girls had their feet **tightly wrapped** so they could not grow properly.

In the middle of the **19th century** many women tried to change their body shape by wearing **corsets**.

Looking cool in 1906.

The corsets pulled in their waists to as little as **45 cm**. This fashion caused lots of **health problems**.

You can look gorgeous, too ...

Tattoos can look great, but what happens if you **change your mind**?

These days you can get tattoos that will **wash off**.

Tattoo artists will paint tattoos for you. You can choose from lots of exotic designs.

Henna tattoos are very popular in the U.K. and U.S.A.

Fingernail art is the latest fashion, especially in the USA and Japan. In Japan, there are even **contests** for nail artists.

Fingernail art is easy to do for **yourself**. You need:

 2 colours of nail polish

 small sticky paper shapes to stick on your nails. You could make these yourself if you like.

✓ Paint your nails with one colour and let it dry thoroughly.

✓ Stick the shapes to your nails.

✓ Paint your nails again with the second colour, and let it dry.

✓ Peel the shapes off.

or for **glittery nails** ...

✓ Paint your nails. Stick small jewels and glitter on before the polish dries.

Don't try this!

Until modern times people used very dangerous substances as cosmetics.

DANGER

In Victorian times, many women used arsenic to make their skin look soft.

Arsenic was often mixed with vinegar and chalk and then eaten to make their faces fashionably pale.

A tonic called Fowler's Solution was used at this time. This also contained arsenic, as people believed it was good for them.

FOWLER'S SOLUTION
POISON! CAUTION!
ALCOHOL 2.4%
FOWLER'S SOLUTION DOSE—For an adult one to five drops.
ANTIDOTE—Evacuate stomach with stomach pump or emetics.
Give hydrated oxide of iron, oil, lard, melted butter, milk and
magnesia in large quantities.
CASE'S PHARMACY, The Rexall Store
Rochester Building, Main and Mulberry Streets, LOGAN, OHIO

We should know better, but we still do things that are dangerous.

If people try to pierce their own ears, or other parts of their bodies they can get painful infections. Always get piercings done by a professional.

Trying to do your own tattoos is even worse. Some people have made themselves very ill.

It is probably better to have temporary tattoos. That way you can change your tattoos when fashions change. Or when you decide to get a new boyfriend or girlfriend!

Death
by
Arsenic

Chapter 1:
My Journal: 1860

At last! I'm going to be a lady's maid. It's what I've always wanted.

The Missus said that I can be maid for Miss Ruth. Miss Ruth is fifteen now. The same age as me.

Miss Pearce will teach me all the things I need to know. I've got to learn to do hair and look after Miss Ruth's clothes.

When I get to be a real grown up lady's maid like Miss Pearce, I will be called Miss Clark, not just Molly.

It's a good job, being a lady's maid. Miss Ruth has been given lots of new clothes.

Her dresses are lovely. Every day I have to help her get into them. She is thin, but she has to have her waist pulled even smaller to fit in the dresses.

It takes a long time to do her hair. Now she is a young lady she looks at the fashion magazines and I have to try to copy the hair styles.

Chapter 2:
Pale and beautiful

Mrs Pearce says I am doing very well. Miss Ruth is pleased with me.

Miss Ruth says that a lady's maid must keep all her mistress's secrets. She says I must never tell anyone what she talks to me about.

Miss Ruth is in love! She is in love with Master John's friend. His name is Michael. He is quite grown up, like Master John who is 20 years old.

Michael comes to visit Master John a lot. When he comes Miss Ruth wears all her best clothes.

Miss Ruth has asked me to go to the chemist. She wants me to buy face cream and paint for her cheeks and lips.

She says I must never tell anyone. Her mama would be very cross if she found out.

I bought some cream to make her face look pale and beautiful.

Chapter 3:
Fowler's Solution

Miss Ruth is not well.

She told me to get a tonic when I got the face cream. I got something special. It is called Fowler's Solution. The man told me to use it once a day.

Miss Ruth said she is much better. But she is sad because Michael does not talk to her.

She has spots on her face, so she uses her cream all the time to hide them.

Miss Ruth's spots are getting worse. She has open sores on her face now. I am the only person to see them.

She covers her face with the cream and her cheeks are pretty and pink, so when the spots are covered she looks very well.

Miss Ruth is using the cream on her lips. She says if it makes her cheeks pink it will do the same for her lips.

Chapter 4:
Dying of love

Miss Ruth is dying of love. She spends much time crying. Michael is courting another girl.

She sends me for more Fowler's Solution two, or even three times a week. I tell her the man says to take it only once a day, but she will not listen.

She says she is sick and weak. Only the solution makes her feel better.

As I read this, I knew what was going to happen. I turned the page and read the words.

'Miss Ruth is dead!'

My great, great grandma never did get to be a lady's maid. It was back to being a house-maid for her.

I wonder if her Missus ever knew what killed Ruth.

I know though. She died from poisoning. Death by arsenic!

Body Art word check

arsenic

corset

cosmetics

Egyptians

face painting

henna

infection

jewellery

marriage ceremonies

Mehndi design

minerals

tattoos

pierce

scar patterns